OHIO VEHICULAR HOMICIDE GUIDE

What You Need to Know Before Going to Court And Before Hiring a Lawyer For Vehicular Homicide in Ohio

Shawn Dominy, Attorney at Law

Rivers Edge Publishing, LLC

THIS GUIDE IS NOT LEGAL ADVICE. Although this guide is written by a lawyer and contains useful information about a legal issue, it is not legal advice, and reading it does not create an attorney-client relationship. The facts and circumstances of every Vehicular Homicide case are different. For a lawyer to give you legal advice, the lawyer needs to know the facts and circumstances of your particular case. Otherwise, it would be like a doctor performing a medical procedure without knowing your symptoms and medical history. If you want legal advice for your specific case, you should hire a lawyer with expertise in the area of Vehicular Homicide defense.

The characters and events portrayed in this book are fictitious. Any similarity to real persons, living or dead, is coincidental and not intended by the author.

ISBN: 978-1-7368732-2-9

Cover design by: Shawn Dominy
Author photo by: Klatte Photography

Printed in the United States of America

Dedicated to Bryan Hawkins and Windy Renee Hall of the Dominy Law Firm for their invaluable contributions to ths guide.

CONTENTS

PREFACE

After fifteen years of representing clients charged with various criminal offenses, I know vehicular homicide cases are, by far, the most devastating for all parties involved.

Attorney Shawn Dominy does an incredible job of dissecting the complexity of the charges and simplifying the process of strategically crafting a defense.

For a person charged with vehicular homicide, this book is a must-read. Understanding both the nature of the charges and the process involved will certainly ease the mind of those facing the potential consequences associated with this alleged crime.

For other attorneys, this book is an outstanding resource to better grasp the essentials in defending individuals charged with the same or similar offenses.

Bravo, Mr. Dominy, for yet another exemplary product."

-Andrew S. Baker, Attorney at Law

INTRODUCTION

Vehicular Homicide is an unintentional offense. Unlike most people charged with criminal offenses, a person charged with Vehicular Homicide did not *intend* to commit a crime. If you were charged with Vehicular Homicide, you know what I mean: you didn't even *expect* an accident to happen. Unfortunately, Vehicular Homicide is considered a 'strict liability' offense: no 'intent' or *mens rea* ('guilty mind') is required.

As a result, people from all walks of life may find themselves charged with Vehicular Homicide. One isolated incident can lead to serious criminal charges for a person who otherwise leads an honorable life. The irony is the punishments for Vehicular Homicide are more severe than many offenses requiring some level of 'intent'. In addition, convictions for Vehicular Homicide cannot be sealed, while the convictions for many crimes requiring some level of 'intent' are eligible for record-sealing.

Vehicular Homicide cases have an emotionally charged atmosphere. The circumstances are distressing for all parties involved. The accused person grapples with the psychological effects of the incident, the potential consequences of the criminal case, and the financial impact of a civil lawsuit. The victim's family mourns the loss of a loved-one, and the criminal case will not bring them back. Because the victim's family may also feel unforgiving, their desire for retribution creates pressure on the prosecutor and the judge. The heightened emotional atmosphere is intensified by pressure from special interest groups, such as MADD, as well as the mandates of victims' rights laws.

Vehicular Homicide requires a swift and effective defense. Given the serious consequences and intense emotional environment, it is crucial that the defendant's lawyer act swiftly *and* effectively. Swift action is necessary because the defense investigation must begin while evidence is available, and memories are fresh. Effective action is necessary because the litigation of these cases is complex. Vehicular Homicide cases involve the intersection of intricate legal issues and complicated scientific evidence.

People charged with Vehicular Homicide have many questions. Being charged with Vehicular Homicide is stressful, and nobody is prepared for it to happen. When it does, a deluge of thoughts overflow your mind.

- What exactly is Vehicular Homicide?
- What are the consequences if I'm found guilty?
- What evidence will be introduced in the case?
- What are the defense strategies?
- What happens at the court appearances?
- Should I plead Guilty or Not Guilty?
- Should I hire a lawyer?
- Does it make a difference which defense lawyer I hire?
- How can I find a good defense lawyer?

I wrote this guide to answer those questions. I am a criminal defense lawyer in Columbus, Ohio, and the focus of my practice is representing clients charged with serious vehicular crimes. With over two decades of experience helping people charged with Vehicular Homicide, I know how empowering it has been for my clients to receive answers to their questions. Reading the information in this guide is a great way to have your questions answered.

After being charged with Vehicular Homicide, the best thing you can do is educate yourself. First, educating yourself will give you an accurate understanding of your situation, which will hopefully reduce the anxiety you're experiencing. Second, learning more will promote avoiding the mistakes commonly made in Vehicular Homicide cases. Third, having this information will help you determine whether you will hire a lawyer. If you choose to hire a lawyer, this guide will assist you in selecting a good lawyer to defend you.

There is a lot of misinformation about Vehicular Homicide cases. Television, movies, and 'urban legends' are full of misunderstandings. Lawyer advertising is not very helpful at clarifying these misunderstandings. All the websites for criminal defense lawyers look about the same, but the reality is all lawyers are not the same. Some have more expertise than others, some get better results than others, and some provide better customer service than others. The problem is it is hard to tell which ones.

This guide will help. In privacy and comfort, you can have your questions answered by reading this guide. *Part One* explains Vehicular Homicide and its consequences, to give you a better understanding of the offense and what you are facing if you are found guilty. *Part Two* discusses evidence in Vehicular Homicide cases, including field sobriety tests, drug recognition evaluations, accident reconstruction, and blood/breath/urine tests. *Part Three* addresses defense strategies for improving the outcomes of Vehicular Homicide cases. *Part Fou*r describes the court process, so you will know what to expect at court appearances.

Part Five provides a framework for evaluating whether you want to plead guilty or fight the charge, as well as whether you want to hire a lawyer. If you decide to hire a lawyer, *Part Five* also identifies resources for researching lawyers, a list of qualifications to look for in defense lawyers, and several questions to ask before hiring a lawyer.

My goal in writing this guide is to provide you with the valuable information you should have before going to court, and before hiring a lawyer, for a Vehicular Homicide case in Ohio.

My hope is that, by reading this guide, you will understand the consequences, the evidence, the strategies, the court process, and the differences among lawyers. With that knowledge, you can make well-informed decisions about how to handle your Vehicular Homicide case.

Shawn Dominy, Attorney at Law

THIS GUIDE IS NOT LEGAL ADVICE

Although this guide is written by a lawyer and contains useful information about a legal issue, it is not legal advice, and reading it does not create an attorney-client relationship. The facts and circumstances of every Vehicular Homicide case are different. For a lawyer to give you legal advice, the lawyer needs to know the facts and circumstances of your particular case. Otherwise, it would be like a doctor performing a medical procedure without knowing your symptoms and medical history. If you want legal advice for your specific case, you should hire a lawyer with expertise in the area of Vehicular Homicide defense.

PART ONE: VEHICULAR HOMICIDE AND ITS CONSEQUENCES

TYPES OF VEHICULAR HOMICIDE CHARGES AND THEIR CONSEQUENCES

The term 'vehicular homicide' is often used to generally describe an offense in which a driver's operation of a motor vehicle causes the death of another person. Ohio law has three separate offenses: (1) Aggravated Vehicular Homicide; (2) Vehicular Homicide; and (3) Vehicular Manslaughter. Each offense has distinct sentences which depend on how the offense is committed and the criminal record of the offender. It is helpful to analyze each offense with two questions:

(1) What does the prosecution have to prove for you to be found guilty?
(2) If you are found guilty, what is the potential sentence?

Aggravated Vehicular Homicide

The prosecution must prove that, while operating a motor vehicle (including a snowmobile, watercraft or aircraft), you caused the death of another person in one of the following ways:

(1) as a proximate result of committing the offense of OVI (**O**perating a **V**ehicle under the **I**nfluence of alcohol and/or drugs)

(2) recklessly

(3) as the proximate result of committing a reckless operation offense in a construction zone

The potential sentence for this offense depends on how the offense is committed (which of those three ways) and the defendant's criminal record.

(1) If this offense is committed by *OVI*, Aggravated Vehicular Homicide is a second-degree felony, and the potential sentence includes a mandatory prison term of two years to eight years, as well as a mandatory license suspension for life.

- This offense is elevated to a first-degree felony, punishable by up to 11 years in prison, if any of the following apply: (1) driving with no license or a suspended license; (2) prior conviction for Vehicular Homicide; or (3) prior conviction for Vehicular Manslaughter or Vehicular Assault.
- This offense is elevated to a first-degree felony, punishable by up to 15 years in prison, if any of the following apply: (1) three or more convictions in the last ten years for operating a vehicle/watercraft/aircraft under the influence of alcohol or drugs; (2) three or more convictions in the last ten years for Vehicular Homicide; (3) three or more convictions in the last ten years for Vehicular Assault; (4) three or more convictions in the last ten years for Involuntary Manslaughter by OVI; (5)

a combination of 1-4 above; or (6) two or more convictions for felony OVI.

- *Reagan Tokes Law*: For an offense which is a first-degree felony or a second-degree felony, the Ohio Department of Rehabilitation and Correction may add prison time to an inmate's sentence for certain misbehavior. The maximum prison time which may be added is 50% of the definite prison term imposed by the judge.

(2) If this offense is committed by *operating a vehicle recklessly*, Aggravated Vehicular Homicide is a third-degree felony, and *the potential sentence* includes a prison term of one year to five years, as well as a mandatory license suspension for three years to life.

- This offense is elevated to a second-degree felony, punishable by up to eight years in prison, if any of the following apply: (1) driving with no license or suspended license; or (2) prior conviction for Vehicular Homicide or any traffic-related homicide, manslaughter, or assault offense.
- The prison term for this offense is mandatory if either of the following apply: (1) prior conviction for Vehicular Homicide or Involuntary Manslaughter; or (2) driving with no license or suspended license.
- The license suspension for this offense is elevated to a suspension for life if the offender has a prior conviction for a traffic-related murder, felonious assault, or attempted murder.

(3) If this offense is committed by *a reckless operation offense in a construction zone*, Aggravated Vehicular Homicide is a third-degree felony, and the *potential sentence* includes a prison term of one year to five years, as well as a mandatory license suspension for three years to life.

- This offense is elevated to a second-degree felony, punishable by up to eight years in prison, if any of the following apply: (1) driving with no license or suspended license; or (2) prior conviction for Vehicular Homicide or any traffic-related homicide, manslaughter, or assault offense.

- The prison term for this offense is mandatory if either of the following apply: (1) prior conviction for Vehicular Homicide or Involuntary Manslaughter; or (2) driving with no license or suspended license.
- The license suspension for this offense is elevated to a suspension for life if the offender has a prior conviction for a traffic-related murder, felonious assault, or attempted murder.

Vehicular Homicide

The prosecution must prove that, while operating a motor vehicle (including a snowmobile, watercraft, or aircraft), you caused the death of another person in one of the following ways: (1) negligently; or (2) as the proximate result of committing a speeding offense in a construction zone.

Vehicular Homicide is a first-degree misdemeanor, and *the potential sentence* includes up to six months in jail and a mandatory license suspension for one year to five years. If this offense is committed as the proximate result of committing a *speeding offense in a construction zone*, there is a minimum mandatory jail sentence of 15 days.

- This offense is elevated to a fourth-degree felony punishable by up to 18 months in prison if either of the following apply: (1) driving with no license or suspended license; or (2) prior conviction for Vehicular Homicide or any traffic-related homicide, manslaughter, or assault offense.
- The license suspension for this offense is elevated to a suspension for two to ten years if the offender has a prior conviction for a traffic-related homicide, manslaughter, or assault offense.
- The license suspension for this offense is elevated to a suspension for three years to life if the offender has a prior conviction for a traffic-related murder, felonious assault, or attempted murder.

Vehicular Manslaughter

The prosecution must prove that, while operating a motor vehicle (including a snowmobile, watercraft, or aircraft), you caused the death of another person as the proximate result of committing a minor misdemeanor traffic offense. The sentence for this offense depends on the defendant's criminal record.

Vehicular Manslaughter is a second-degree misdemeanor, and *the potential sentence* includes up to 90 days in jail and a mandatory license suspension for six months to three years.

- This offense is elevated to a first-degree misdemeanor, punishable by up to six months in jail, if either of the following apply: (1) driving with no license or suspended license; or (2) prior conviction for Vehicular Homicide or any traffic-related homicide, manslaughter, or assault offense.
- The license suspension for this offense is elevated to a suspension for one year to five years if the offender has a prior conviction for a traffic-related murder, felonious assault, or attempted murder.

CIVIL CONSEQUENCES OF VEHICULAR HOMICIDE

When you are charged with the crime of vehicular homicide, the estate of the victim typically files a civil lawsuit against you. You will then have both a criminal case and a civil case: two independent cases with independent resolutions. For example, in the cases of O.J. Simpson, he was found not guilty of murder in the criminal case, but he was found liable for wrongful death in the civil case and ordered to pay $8.5 million to the Goldman family.

Part One has explained vehicular homicide charges and their consequences. Before you incur any of those consequences, the evidence must first prove you are guilty of vehicular homicide. Evidence for vehicular homicide cases is discussed in *Part Two*.

OVI CHARGES IN AGGRAVATED VEHICULAR HOMICIDE CASES

As described above, one way to commit the offense of Aggravated Vehicular Homicide is causing the death of another person as a proximate result of committing the offense of OVI. Drunk driving is known by many acronyms. In Ohio, it's called **OVI**, which stands for **O**perating a **V**ehicle under the **I**nfluence of alcohol and/or drugs.

There are two general types of OVI charges, which means there are two general ways a prosecutor can try to prove your guilt: OVI "impaired" and OVI "per se".

O.V.I. "Impaired". The prosecution must prove you *operated a vehicle '**under the influence**' of alcohol and/or drugs*. You are considered 'under the influence' if the alcohol or drug affected your nervous system, brain, or muscles to noticeably impair your actions, reactions, or mental processes - which *impaired* your ability to operate a vehicle. For the "impaired" charge, the level of alcohol or drugs does not matter. All that matters is the alcohol or drugs impaired your ability to drive.

OVI "Per Se". The prosecution must prove you *operated a vehicle* *with a **prohibited concentration** of alcohol or drugs in your blood, breath, or urine*. For the "per se" charge, it does not matter whether the alcohol or drug was impairing your ability to drive. All that matters is you had a prohibited concentration of alcohol or drugs in your system (you were over the 'legal limit') when you operated the vehicle. The prohibited concentrations for alcohol and drugs are listed in the table below.

Prohibited Concentrations: OVI "Per Se"

Substance	Blood	Urine	Breath
Alcohol	.080 %	.110 %	.080 %
Amphetamine / Methamphetamine	100 ng	500 ng	
Cocaine	50 ng	150 ng	
Heroin	50 ng	2,000 ng	
Heroin Metabolite	10 ng	10 ng	
L.S.D.	10 ng	25 ng	
Marijuana	2 ng	10 ng	
Marijuana Metabolite	50 ng	35 ng	
MJ Metabolite & Under the Influence	5 ng	15 ng	

Consequences of an OVI Conviction

If you are convicted of OVI, there are mandatory minimum sentences a judge *must* impose, and there is a broad range of punishments a judge *may* impose. The minimum and maximum sentences increase based upon the number of prior OVI convictions within the last ten years and the last 20 years. The following table summarizes the potential OVI sentences in Ohio.

Potential Sentences for OVI in Ohio

Offense Number	Jail Term	Fine & Costs	License Suspension	Time w/o Privileges	Immobilize or Forfeit Car?	Yellow Plates & Interlock
First	3 days to 6 months	$375 to $1,075	1 year to 3 years	15 days	No	Maybe
Second	10 days to 6 months	$525 to $1,625	1 year to 7 years	45 days	90 days	Yes
Third	30 days to 12 months	$850 to $2,750	2 years to 12 years	180 days	Forfeiture	Yes
Felony (First)	60 days to 30 months	$1,350 - $10,500	3 years to Life	3 years	Forfeiture	Yes
Felony (Second)	60 days to 5 years	$1,350 - $10,500	3 years to Life	3 years	Forfeiture	Yes

Notes about this table: First, if the conviction is for a "high test" (blood alcohol concentration of .170 or higher) or for a "test refusal with prior conviction" (in the last 20 years), the minimum mandatory jail term is doubled. Second, the table is a very simplified summary of OVI sentencing at the time this guide was written; there are variations to these sentences. Third, OVI sentencing is subject to change at any time by the Ohio legislature.

Consecutive Sentencing. If you are convicted of Aggravated Vehicular Homicide and OVI, the judge can sentence you on both charges and order that the terms of incarceration run consecutively (one after-the-other).

ADMINISTRATIVE LICENSE SUSPENSIONS

In vehicular homicide cases which also involve allegations of OVI, there may be two different types of suspensions:

(1) if you are asked to take a breath/blood/urine test and you either refuse the test <u>or</u> test 'over the limit', an *Administrative License Suspension* (ALS) is immediately imposed by the Ohio Bureau of Motor Vehicles (BMV)

(2) if you are found guilty of vehicular homicide or OVI, a *Court Suspension* is imposed by the judge.

If you are subjected to an ALS, the court may grant limited driving privileges. There is, however, a waiting period ("hard time") during which the court cannot grant limited driving privileges.

The length of the ALS, and the waiting period for driving privileges, depends on whether you refused to take the test or tested 'over the limit', as well as the number of prior OVI convictions and test refusals on your record. The following tables summarize Administrative License Suspensions in Ohio:

ALS for Test Refusal

Refusals/Convictions in the last 10 Years	Length of Suspension	Waiting Period for Driving Privileges
No priors	One year	30 days
One prior	Two years	90 days
Two priors	Three years	One year
Three priors	Five years	Three years

ALS for Test 'Over the Limit'

Refusals/Convictions in the last 10 Years	Length of Suspension	Waiting Period for Driving Privileges
No priors	90 days	15 days
One prior	One year	45 days
Two priors	Two years	180 days
Three priors	Three years	Three years

Administrative License Suspensions are part of Ohio's 'implied consent' law. That law states any driver who operates a vehicle in the state of Ohio implicitly consents to take a blood/breath/urine test for alcohol and/or drugs if the driver is arrested for OVI. 'Implied consent' also applies to any driver who is unconscious or otherwise in a condition rendering the person incapable of refusing.

A driver license is considered property, and no person can be deprived of property without due process of law. Accordingly, if your license is being suspended, you have the right to due process of law. That means the ALS is only valid if the officer followed the procedures required by Ohio law. Officers do not always follow the required procedures.

Your right to due process also means you must be given notice of the suspension and an opportunity to appeal the suspension. There are two ways to challenge the ALS:

1. Motion Appealing the ALS
2. Motion to Terminate the ALS

The most common attacks on the ALS are discussed later, in the section for *Defenses to the Administrative License Suspension.* It should be noted, however, that a successful challenge to the ALS may be in vain, as a judge can also order that you not operate a vehicle as a condition of bond.

Case Example

In a recent case of ours, the officer gave our client an ALS notice but did not complete the section where the officer states the reasons for asking our client to take a test. Ohio law requires the officer to give the defendant a 'completed' form, and the form given to our client was not 'completed'. We appealed, and the ALS was terminated at the arraignment.

PART TWO: EVIDENCE IN VEHICULAR HOMICIDE CASES

INITIAL CONTACT WITH LAW ENFORCEMENT AND THE MIRANDA MYTH

In most vehicular homicide cases, your initial contact with a law enforcement officer occurs soon after the accident. That contact may occur at the accident scene, or that contact may occur at the hospital. Officers do not need a justification to interact with you as part of an accident investigation.

Officers typically ask questions about the accident, including inquiries about your driving and how the crash occurred. Officers may also ask about consuming alcohol, ingesting illegal drugs, and taking prescription medications. If the officer suspects you are responsible for the death of another person, the officer will record your answers in a report, and probably on video, for later use in court.

The most common misunderstanding about criminal cases is probably the impact of *Miranda* warnings. Television and movies would have us believe the officer's failure to issue *Miranda* warnings means the whole case is thrown out.

If you make statements that incriminate you (e.g., "I drank 19 beers"), the prosecution would like to use those statements against you in court. The principle from the Miranda case is this: if you are in custody and the officer does not give you *Miranda* warnings, any statements you make while in custody cannot be used against you at trial. That is the impact of *Miranda*. The statements are thrown out, but not the entire case.

When you are 'in custody' is a gray area. An Ohio Supreme Court case states you do not have to be formally arrested to be 'in custody'. When the situation changes from a routine accident investigation to a vehicular homicide investigation with you as the suspect, you may be 'in custody'.

Your attorney should investigate the circumstances surrounding any statements you made to the police. If you made incriminating statements while you were 'in custody' and the officer did not issue *Miranda* warnings, your attorney should file a motion to suppress (throw out) those statements.

FIELD SOBRIETY TESTS

If the officer suspects you are under the influence of alcohol or drugs, and if you are physically capable, the officer almost always administers field sobriety tests. You are not required to take those tests, and there are no penalties for declining the tests. Officers do not tell people this, so nearly everybody takes them.

The *three standardized field sobriety tests* are designed to help the officer determine whether to charge you with a crime. The tests also are used by the prosecution to argue your performance on the tests is circumstantial evidence that you were under the influence or 'over the limit'.

Horizontal Gaze Nystagmus Test. The officer has you follow a pen or a finger with your eyes. During this test, the officer is looking for an involuntary jerking of the eyeball (nystagmus) because studies show that alcohol, and some drugs, increase the presence of nystagmus. During this six-part test, the officer scores a "clue" each time nystagmus is observed. There are six possible "clues", and the presence of four or more "clues" suggests your blood alcohol content is .08 or higher. Even if you are physically incapable of performing the other tests, this test is often still administered, even on a stretcher or in a hospital bed.

Walk And Turn Test. The officer instructs you to stand on a line, walk nine heel-to-toe steps down the line, turn around, and walk nine heel-to-toe steps back. As you perform the test, the officer looks for "clues". There are eight possible "clues", and the presence of two or more "clues" indicates a probability that your blood alcohol content is .08 or higher. The eight "clues" are:

- lose your balance during the instructions
- start too early
- fail to touch heel-to-toe
- stop walking
- step off the line
- raise your arms for balance
- turn improperly
- take an incorrect number of steps

One Leg Stand Test. The officer instructs you to raise one foot approximately six inches off the ground, stand on the other leg with your arms at your sides, and count aloud for 30 seconds. As you perform the test, the officer scores "clues". There are four possible "clues", and the presence of two or more "clues" indicates a probability that your blood alcohol content is .08 or higher. The four clues are:

- sway
- use your arms for balance
- hop
- put your foot down

Non-Standardized Tests. In addition to the three standardized field sobriety tests, some officers also administer non-standardized tests, such as counting backward, reciting part of the alphabet, and touching your nose with your eyes closed and your head tilted back. These tests have no standardized procedure, and no studies show a correlation between these tests and being under the influence or 'over the limit'.

Your attorney should scrutinize the field sobriety tests. If your attorney has training in field sobriety testing, he or she can review the cruiser video and cross-examine the officer to determine if the officer made mistakes administering the tests. I have had many cross-examinations reveal the officer made mistakes, which resulted in the tests being thrown out. Even if the tests are not thrown out, effective cross-examination of the officer can show why the tests really do not measure intoxication.

Are Field Sobriety Tests Fair?

When officers administer field sobriety tests, they do not tell subjects what "clues" will be scored, and they do not give subjects an opportunity to practice. What other tests do people take where they are not told what is being graded and are not permitted to study? If standing on one leg and walking heel-to-toe can predict driving ability, why aren't those tests part of the driver's license examination?

DRUG RECOGNITION EVALUATIONS

If a law enforcement officer suspects a driver is under the influence of drugs, the officer may administer a drug recognition evaluation. Unlike the field sobriety tests, which are conducted *before* a driver is arrested, a drug recognition evaluation is administered *after* the driver's arrest. The purposes of the evaluation are to determine whether the driver is under the influence of a drug and predict what class of drug is causing the driver's impairment.

The evaluations must conducted by an officer who is certified as a Drug Recognition Evaluator, also called a Drug Recognition Expert (DRE). To become a DRE, an officer must complete the 72-hour 'Drug Examination and Classification Program'. The DRE program has been used in Ohio since the 1990s, but there are relatively few certified DREs in Ohio, so arresting officers often call-in a DRE to perform a drug recognition evaluation.

The drug recognition evaluation, typically administered at a police station, is a 12-step assessment. Some of the steps in the evaluation repeat tests which were likely performed before the arrest. The 12 steps are:

1. Breath Alcohol Test
2. Interview of the Arresting Officer
3. Preliminary Examination and First Pulse
4. Eye Examination: Horizontal Gaze Nystagmus, Vertical Nystagmus, and Lack Of Convergence
5. Divided Attention Tests: Modified Romberg, Walk And Turn, One Leg Stand, Finger-To-Nose

6. Vital Signs and Second Pulse
7. Pupil Size: reaction to light and rebound dilation
8. Muscle Tone
9. Injection Sites and Third Pulse
10. Subject's Statements and Other Observations
11. Analysis and Opinions of the Evaluator
12. Toxicological Examination: blood and/or urine sample

The evaluations are subject to confirmation bias, some components of the evaluation are not related to drug impairment, and the protocol was not subjected to critical peer review. Subsequent validation studies show the evaluations are ineffective, resulting in false-positives and false-negatives.

HOW OFFICERS DECIDE IF YOU WILL BE CHARGED WITH VEHICULAR HOMICIDE

At the conclusion of the initial investigation, the officer decides whether you are going to be charged with vehicular homicide. If you are going to be charged, the officer typically arrests you and issues a complaint charging you with vehicular homicide.

Some people believe they were not "arrested" because they were not taken to a police station or jail. An 'arrest' actually occurs when the officer decides you are going to be charged and detains you (usually, but not always, in handcuffs) to give you a complaint. To justify arresting you, the officer must have probable cause to believe you committed the offense.

The decision to arrest you is supposed to be based upon the 'totality of the circumstances'. In addition to considering all the evidence indicating you *are* guilty of the offense, the officer should also consider all the evidence indicating you are *not* guilty of the offense. The evidence includes everything the officer observes at the accident scene, while speaking with you, and when the field sobriety tests are administered.

Your lawyer should look closely at the circumstances leading to the arrest. If the arrest was not justified by probable cause, any evidence obtained after the arrest is excluded, including any blood/

breath/urine tests and any statements you made to the officer.

If your charge is a felony, the officer may or may not serve you with a complaint after the initial investigation. If a complaint is issued for a felony, the case is initially heard in the *Municipal Court*. However, permanent jurisdiction for the case is with the *Common Pleas Court*.

For your case to be initiated in the *Common Pleas Court*, the case must be heard by a grand jury. The grand jury reviews the evidence and decides whether you will be formally charged in the *Common Pleas Court*. If you are charged, the grand jury issues an indictment: a document informing you of the charge(s). This topic is further discussed in *Part Four: The Court Process for Vehicular Homicide Cases*.

ACCIDENT INVESTIGATION AND RECONSTRUCTION

In every vehicular homicide case, an officer conducts an accident investigation. In most vehicular homicide cases, an officer (or civilian) performs accident reconstruction. Both are important in a vehicular homicide case.

Accident Investigation. The purpose of accident investigation is to collect evidence. The accident investigation is typically conducted by a police officer soon after the crash occurs. The officer should have training and experience in accident investigations. Preferably, the officer also should have some training in accident reconstruction, as the evidence collected will likely be used for accident reconstruction.

The officer conducting the accident investigation collects the following types of evidence:

- Witness statements
- Accident site conditions: sight lines, lighting, visibility, signage, debris scattering
- Road surface conditions: skid marks, critical speed scuffs (yaw marks), gouges scrapes
- Accident location points: point of impact, final resting positions, witness perspectives, operators' perspectives
- Measurements: base-line, triangulation, and electronic
- Exterior vehicle conditions: damage, defects, paint transfer, plastic transfer, vehicle fluid transfer, vehicle fluid trails
- Interior vehicle conditions: seat belts, air bags, seat position, damage, defects, bodily fluids, skin transfer, fabric transfer
- Passenger conditions: injuries, clothing, intoxication
- Evidence of operation: chest injury, face injury, clothing fibers, seatbelt abrasions, teeth impressions, bodily fluids, fingerprints, DNA

The evidence should be thoroughly documented in photographs and videos.

Accident Reconstruction. The purpose of accident reconstruction is to scientifically evaluate the collected evidence to ascertain how the crash occurred and determine the cause of the accident. An accident reconstruction should be performed by a person certified in accident reconstruction.

The person performing the accident reconstruction does the following:

- Study diagrams of the accident scene and accident site
- Determine points of first possible perception, actual perception, no escape, operator action, impact, and final resting position
- Utilize a drag sled or accelerometer to determine the road surface's drag factor
- Apply manual algebraic equations, such as conservation of momentum
- Employ computer-assisted formulas
- Implement computer-generated simulations
- Consider vehicle mechanical defects or failures, including any relevant vehicle recalls
- Evaluate human factors to account for the actions and inactions of drivers which may have played a role in the crash, including perception-reaction time
- Analyze airbag control modules, diesel engine event data recorders, powertrain control modules, global positioning systems, and vehicle cameras
- Interpret 'black box' reports from Electronic Data Recorder (EDR) systems, also known as Crash Data Retrieval (CDR) systems

'Black Box' Reports. An Electronic Data Recorder (EDR) receives data from various systems in the vehicle. The EDR continuously records the received data, but the data is not saved for reporting use unless there is a crash. The recording then saves the data from the time of the crash and several seconds before the crash.

The data from the EDR is downloaded and reported in software developed by Bosch, so the reports are often called 'Bosch Reports', although a couple manufacturers use other programs. The data in the report varies among different vehicles, but most reports include vehicle speed, engine RPM, use of brakes, deployment of air bags, and use of seat belt.

Your attorney should thoroughly review the accident investigation and the accident reconstruction. Both the investigation and the reconstruction are prone to errors which can have an impact on the strength of the case. Some of those errors are addressed in *Part Three: Defense Strategies for Vehicular Homicide Cases.*

CORONER'S REPORT

In all vehicular homicide cases, there should be a coroner's report. The report is sometimes called a Pathology Report or Autopsy Report. In Ohio, a coroner is a medical doctor employed by the county and is elected by the county's voters. The county coroner often appoints deputy coroners (mostly forensic pathologists) to conduct autopsies.

An autopsy is a surgical examination of a corpse conducted for the purpose of determining the manner and cause of death. The autopsy includes an exterior inspection of the body, with weights and measurements, as well as an inspection of the body's organs and tissues. The pathologist notes injuries and abnormalities, and also obtains samples of bodily fluids. The bodily fluids are sent to a forensic laboratory for examination.

The coroner or pathologist conducting the autopsy prepares a written report. The report summarizes the process followed in the autopsy and the conclusions reached regarding the manner and cause of death. In addition to the Coroner's Report, there should also be a death certificate, a toxicology report from the bodily fluids, bench notes, witness reports, photographs, and possibly an audio recording.

Your attorney should obtain the Coroner's Report and all the associated documents. The report and documents may reveal shortcomings in the examination which render the conclusions invalid. The documents may also show the victim was under the influence or otherwise call into question whether your alleged reckless/negligent/intoxicated driving was the cause of death.

TESTING BLOOD/ BREATH/URINE TO MEASURE ALCOHOL AND DRUG LEVELS

When too much alcohol, or another drug, gets to your brain, it impairs abilities necessary for driving. Those abilities include vision, coordination, and reactions. Although the same amount of alcohol or drugs may have very different effects on different people, the 'legal limit' for everyone is the same.

Ohio's OVI "per se" laws make it illegal to operate a vehicle with a prohibited amount of alcohol or drugs. Therefore, law enforcement must have a way to measure the amount of alcohol and drugs in a person's system. The most accurate measurement probably would be obtained by testing brain tissue, but even 'tough on crime' politicians would not recommend that method. In Ohio, alcohol and drug levels are measured in blood, breath, and urine.

Blood tests are considered to be the most accurate tests because they 'directly' measure the level of alcohol and drugs in your blood. In Ohio, there are two types of blood tests: (1) crime lab tests, and (2) hospital tests. Crime lab blood tests do not require expert testimony but must comply with regulations by the Ohio Department of Health to be admissible. Hospital blood tests do not need to comply with those regulations but do require expert testimony to make them admissible.

Blood tests can be done against your will. An officer may have your blood forcibly drawn if the officer obtains a search warrant, or if there are "exigent circumstances": a compelling need for the blood and no time to secure a warrant. For cases involving blood tests, there are many issues for your lawyer to explore, including the manner in which the blood is drawn, collected, sealed, labeled, stored, transported, and tested. Problems in any of those areas can lead to the blood test being thrown out or having its accuracy doubted.

Breath tests indirectly measure blood alcohol content. Alcohol in your blood makes its way into your lungs and is expired when you exhale. Rather than go through the hassle of drawing your blood, officers can more conveniently measure the alcohol in your breath by having you blow into a machine.

For the breath test to be admissible in court, it must be conducted using an approved machine, and the machine must be maintained in compliance with a long list of regulations. Your lawyer should check the records for the breath-testing machine to determine if the police department failed to comply with any of those regulations. If the police department did not substantially comply with the regulations, the breath test is thrown out. Your lawyer also should explore any possible explanations for why the machine did not produce an accurate result in your test.

Urine tests, like breath tests, indirectly measure blood alcohol levels. Unlike breath tests, urine tests also measure drug levels. The concentration of alcohol or drugs in your urine is not the same as the concentration in your blood, so the alcohol and drug limits are different for urine. Most states do not use urine tests as evidence because alcohol or drugs may remain in urine long after they have dissipated from the blood and are no longer affecting your ability to drive. Nevertheless, Ohio uses urine testing in vehicular homicide cases.

For a urine test to be admissible in court, the test must be conducted in compliance with Ohio regulations. If the urine sample was not collected, handled, transported, tested, and stored in compliance with those regulations, the test is thrown out. If the urine test is not thrown out, you may still introduce evidence to show why the result was not accurate.

Breath Testing in Ohio

Ohio is unique in its approach to the litigation of breath test cases. In the 1984 case of *State v. Vega*, the Ohio Supreme Court held that a defendant may not make a general attack on the reliability and validity of the breath-testing machine. Some courts interpret *Vega* to prohibit any attack.

In the 2013 case of State v. Lancaster, an Ohio Court held that a defendant may attack the reliability of the specific testing procedure and the particular equipment used for the breath test. The judge concluded that, although a breath-testing machine is presumed to be reliable, the defense proved that the Intoxilyzer 8000 machines used in those cases are not reliable. As a result, tests on those particular machines are not admissible as evidence. I was defense counsel in this case, and you can read more about the case on the Dominy Law Firm blog.

Should I Take the Test?

When a driver is arrested in Ohio for a charge related to OVI, the driver is asked to submit to a breath/blood/urine test. Some lawyers advise everyone to refuse the test. That is not always good advice. Before taking or refusing a test, the following possible outcomes should be considered:

- If you *take* the test and the result is *over* the prohibited amount:

(a) your license will be suspended for 90 days (or longer if you have prior OVI convictions or test refusals)

(b) you will be charged with OVI "per se" and OVI "impaired"

(c) the prosecution will use the results of the test against you in court.

- If you *take* the test and the result is *under* the prohibited amount:

(a) your license will not be suspended

(b) you will not be charged with OVI "per se" – only OVI "impaired"

(b) the results of the test will not be damaging in court

- If you *refuse* the test:

(a) your license will be suspended for one year (or longer if you have prior OVI convictions or test refusals)

(b) you will not be charged with OVI "per se" – only OVI "impaired"

(b) the prosecution will not have test results to use against you in court.

- If you *refuse* the test, you may have blood drawn involuntarily. This can be the worst of both worlds if the result is 'over the limit': your license is suspended for refusing the test, and the prosecution will use the blood test results in court.

- For some people, there is additional punishment for refusing the breath/blood/urine test. If you have a prior OVI conviction within 20 years, refusal of the test is a separate offense. If you are a commercial driver with a CDL, you face additional sanctions for refusing the test. If you are on probation for OVI, refusing is typically a violation of probation.

PART THREE: DEFENSE STRATEGIES FOR VEHICULAR HOMICIDE CASES

Every vehicular homicide case is unique, and the defense must be tailored to the facts of the case. Nevertheless, good defense lawyers are aware of commonly used strategies which are effective. The strategies listed below do not address every possible defense; just some which are common. Some defenses address the allegation you were 'under the influence', some address the allegation you were 'over the limit', and others address the allegation your driving caused the accident, which caused the death of another person.

INITIATE THE DEFENSE INVESTIGATION QUICKLY

One strategy which is common to nearly every case is starting the defense as early as possible. The crash scene changes, witnesses disappear, and memories fade. The defense investigation should include taking photographs and video of the scene, generating maps of the accident location and driving route, conducting witness interviews, and gathering medical records. It should also include requesting other records, obtaining surveillance videos, and contacting your insurance company. Once the court case is initiated, your lawyer should file a *Demand for Discovery* and put the prosecution on notice to preserve evidence.

As the client, your assignment is to complete a report for your lawyer. You should prepare the report soon after the accident, while the incident is fresh in your mind. The report should include everything you can remember about the crash and the investigation. It should also include a summary of that day and even your entire week. In addition to the report, you also should make a list of witnesses and their contact information, notes about your vehicle condition, and a list of your medical conditions and medications. It is also beneficial to prepare a biographical history so your attorney can personalize you to the prosecutor and judge (and possibly a jury).

DEFENSES TO THE ALLEGATION YOU WERE 'UNDER THE INFLUENCE'

For a charge of Aggravated Vehicular Homicide based on the charge of OVI 'impaired', the prosecution must prove you operated a vehicle 'under the influence' of alcohol and/or drugs. The level of alcohol or drugs does not matter. All that matters is the alcohol or drugs impaired your ability to drive.

Proving the OVI 'Impaired charge relies heavily on observations of witnesses, primarily police officers. The proof comes from the cumulative effect of the individual pieces of evidence, like ingredients in a recipe (e.g., accident, slurred speech, poor performance on sobriety tests, etc.). The defenses are designed to show there are incorrect or missing ingredients. Not every case involves every defense: we use only the defenses applicable to that particular case.

Below are defenses to the allegation you were 'under the influence':

1. Driving: lack proof you were the operator of the vehicle
2. Alcohol or drugs consumed after the accident
3. Interaction with officer: no odor of alcohol
4. Interaction with officer: no slurred speech

5. Interaction with officer: no glassy/bloodshot eyes
6. Interaction with officer: no admission of consuming alcohol or drugs
7. Interaction with officer: no problem with mental faculties
8. Interaction with officer: no problem with physical coordination
9. Interaction with officer: no problem with divided attention
10. No evidence of alcohol or drugs/drug paraphernalia in vehicle
11. Field sobriety tests: not admissible due to lack of compliance with training manual
12. Field sobriety tests: not reliable due to faulty administration
13. Field sobriety tests: good performance from common sense perspective despite observation of technical 'clues'
14. Field sobriety tests: unrelated to impaired driving ability
15. Field sobriety tests: medical condition affected ability to perform tests
16. Field sobriety tests: non-standardized tests have no correlation with intoxication
17. Field sobriety tests: non-standardized tests inadmissible under rules of evidence
18. Drug recognition evaluations: 12-steps not properly implemented
19. Drug recognition evaluations: failure to comply with certification requirement
20. Drug recognition evaluations: components unrelated to driving impairment
21. No problems with balance
22. No problems with coordination
23. No problems following instructions
24. Arrest unlawful: officer did not have probable cause to believe driver was under the influence
25. Arrest unlawful: officer outside jurisdiction
26. Statements made to officer inadmissible due to lack of *Miranda* warnings
27. Statements made to officer inaccurately reported or taken out of context
28. Fatigue has symptoms which can be mistaken for intoxication

29. Medical conditions may have symptoms which can be mistaken for intoxication
30. Ambien use negates the *actus reus* requirement; the act of driving is involuntary
31. Confirmation bias: officer jumped to conclusion and looked for evidence to confirm conclusion
32. Officer discounted evidence inconsistent with intoxication
33. Officer under pressure to make arrest
34. Refusal of chemical test: no advice or improper advice given regarding consequences of refusing test
35. Refusal of chemical test: no notification of right to appeal or independent chemical test
36. Refusal of chemical test: officer's claim of refusal inaccurate
37. Refusal of chemical test: inability to take test is not a refusal
38. Refusal of chemical test: enhancement of penalty improper because prior OVI convictions 'invalid'
39. Evidence destroyed after requested by defense
40. Speedy trial rights violated

DEFENSES TO THE ALLEGATION YOU WERE 'OVER THE LIMIT'

For a charge of Aggravated Vehicular Homicide based on the charge of OVI 'per se', the prosecution must prove you operated a vehicle with a prohibited concentration of alcohol or drugs in your blood, breath, or urine. It does not matter whether the alcohol or drug was impairing your ability to drive. All that matters is you had a prohibited concentration of alcohol or drugs in your system (you were over the 'legal limit') when the crash occurred.

To prove your alcohol and/or drug level was 'over the limit', the prosecution will introduce the results of a breath test, blood test, or urine test. The defenses to the allegation you were 'over the limit' generally aim to exclude the test results from evidence or explain why the test results were inaccurate.

Below are defenses to the allegation you were 'over the limit':

Breath Tests

1. BAC was not 'over the limit' at the time of operating the vehicle due to rising BAC
2. Breath temperature was not measured, and breath temperature affected test result
3. Driver's breathing pattern affected test result
4. Cell phone in area of breath test caused radio frequency interference
5. Breath-testing machine plugged into outlet with other electrical devices
6. Driver had foreign substance in mouth at time of breath test
7. Medical condition affected accuracy of test
8. Ambient air contained alcohol which inflated test result
9. Breath-testing machine not properly maintained
10. Officer did not conduct 20-minute observation period before test
11. Invalid sample not followed by 20-minute observation period
12. Records for breath-testing machine not maintained for prescribed period
13. Instrument check not performed every seven days
14. Instrument check did not yield valid result
15. Radio frequency interference check not performed every seven days
16. Instrument check solution used beyond expiration date
17. Instrument check solution not refrigerated when not in use
18. Instrument check solution container not retained for prescribed period
19. Breath test operator did not have valid permit
20. Breath-testing machine senior operator for maintenance did not have valid permit
21. Breath-testing machine not in proper working order

Blood & Urine Tests

22. No search warrant and no exception to search warrant requirement
23. Defective search warrant
24. Procedure manual for test not on file in analytical testing area
25. Procedures used by laboratory not scientifically valid
26. Procedures for analytical testing not followed
27. Technique used for testing not approved by Ohio Department of Health
28. Instrument(s) used for testing were not calibrated daily
29. Instrument(s) used for testing failed calibration
30. Laboratory records not maintained for prescribed period
31. Sample not refrigerated when not in transit
32. Sample not sealed and labeled as required by Ohio Department of Health
33. Chain of custody for sample not properly documented and retained
34. Sample not retained for additional testing
35. Laboratory did not successfully complete national proficiency testing program
36. Analyst did not have a valid laboratory technician or director permit
37. Laboratory report inadequate
38. Medical condition affected result of test
39. Medication affected result of test
40. Analyst error in testing sequence
41. Instrument used for testing has internal contamination
42. Balance instruments not calibrated
43. Internal standards, standards, and controls invalid
44. Uncertainty in measurement not calculated
45. Mass spectrometer spectral library used for confirmation invalid
46. Blood draw not conducted by qualified individual

47. Blood draw not conducted with sterile dry needle into vacuum container
48. Blood collected in container without solid anticoagulant
49. Urine sample not collected in accordance with Ohio regulations
50. Urine alcohol level at time of operating vehicle was below the 'legal limit' due to pooling of alcohol in urine

DEFENSES TO THE ALLEGATION YOUR DRIVING CAUSED THE ACCIDENT

For all charges of vehicular homicide, the prosecution must prove your operation of a motor vehicle caused the death of another person. The proof comes primarily from the accident investigation and accident reconstruction which concluded your driving caused the crash. The defenses are designed to show the accident investigation and reconstruction were flawed, so the conclusions were incorrect. Below are defenses to the allegation your driving caused the accident:

1. Not all evidence collected and/or photographed
2. Measurements inaccurate or incorrect
3. Diagrams of accident scene inaccurate
4. Failure to investigate signage near accident site
5. Evidence contaminated by moving debris or objects
6. Evidence contaminated by moving vehicles
7. Investigation conducted by officer without proper training and experience
8. Biased accident investigation
9. Eyewitness statements inaccurate due to flawed perception or memory
10. Client statement reported inaccurately or taken out of context
11. No accident reconstruction conducted

12. Reconstructionist lacked training and credentials
13. Reconstructionist had vested interest in conclusion: non-scientific conclusions
14. Misinterpreted exterior vehicle conditions, such as damage, paint transfer, plastic transfer, vehicle fluid transfer, and vehicle fluid trails
15. Misinterpreted interior vehicle conditions, such as seat belts, air bags, seat position, damage, bodily fluids, skin transfer, and fabric transfer
16. No investigation of relevant vehicle recalls
17. Client vehicle's mechanical defect or failure caused the accident
18. Other driver's mechanical defect or failure caused the accident
19. Other driver's intoxication caused the accident
20. Other driver's recklessness or negligence caused the accident
21. Other driver's medical condition caused the accident
22. Other driver's medical condition caused the death
23. Client's medical condition caused the accident
24. Reconstruction failed to properly account for sight lines and visibility
25. Reconstruction based on inaccurate witness' or operators' perspectives
26. Inaccurate determination of points of first possible perception, actual perception, no escape, operator action, impact, and final resting position
27. Failure to properly evaluate human factors which may have played a role in the crash, including perception-reaction time
28. Misinterpreted skid marks, yaw marks, gouges, and scrapes
29. Use of yaw marks invalid due to braking or acceleration when mark was created
30. Drag sled or accelerometer not used to determine road surface's drag factor
31. Misinterpreted exterior vehicle conditions, such as damage, paint transfer, plastic transfer, vehicle fluid transfer, and vehicle fluid trails
32. Misinterpreted interior vehicle conditions, such as seat belts,

air bags, seat position, damage, bodily fluids, skin transfer, and fabric transfer

33. 'Rules of thumb' used; not scientific analysis and mathematical calculations
34. Calculations based on inaccurate interpretation of debris scattering
35. Formulas generated results which defy laws of physics
36. Equations excessively sensitive to minor evidence/input data inaccuracies
37. Equations incorrectly applied: guessing and/or adjustments made to equation
38. Computer-assisted formulas yielded inaccurate results due to incorrect data
39. Results of equations inconsistent with witness observations
40. Computer-generated accident simulation was one presumed scenario, and alternate scenarios not considered
41. Incorrect interpretation of data in 'Bosch' reports from Crash Data Retrieval (CDR) systems, also called Electronic Data Recorders (EDR)
42. Speed in CDR Report invalid due to weather conditions.
43. Reconstruction ignored lack of operation evidence: expected injuries, clothing fibers, seatbelt abrasions, teeth impressions, bodily fluids, fingerprints, and DNA
44. Errors in autopsy led to incorrect conclusion about cause of death
45. Inaccurate analysis of debris spread and body resting place in pedestrian strike

DEFENSES TO THE ADMINISTRATIVE LICENSE SUSPENSION

If you refuse a breath/blood/urine test or test 'over the limit', an Administrative License Suspension (ALS) is imposed by the Ohio Bureau of Motor Vehicles. When you are subjected to an ALS, you have the right to due process of law. That means the ALS is only valid if the officer followed the procedures required by Ohio law. That also means you must be given the opportunity to appeal the suspension.

The lawyers at the Dominy Law Firm created a list of defenses to the ALS called '*50 Ways to Leave Your ALS Lover*'. The defenses are asserted by filing a motion appealing the ALS and a separate motion to terminate the ALS.

Here are the top 10 defenses to the ALS:

1. Officer did not have reasonable grounds to believe driver was under the influence
2. Officer did not properly advise driver of consequences for taking or refusing a chemical test
3. Driver did not refuse a chemical test or test result was not 'over the limit'
4. Officer did not have a witness while reading the ALS form
5. Officer did not notify driver of the rights to appeal and independent chemical test
6. Officer completed the ALS report incorrectly
7. Officer did not give a complete ALS report to the driver
8. Officer did not have the ALS report sworn properly
9. Officer did not send the ALS report to the BMV, or the court, within 48 hours
10. Driver's initial appearance in court not held within five business days

The Administrative License Suspension is addressed at the Arraignment. The arraignment and the other stages of the court process are discussed in *Part Four*.

PART FOUR: THE COURT PROCESS FOR VEHICULAR HOMICIDE CASES

Misdemeanor or Felony

The first part of the court process will depend on whether you are charged with a misdemeanor or a felony. If you are charged with a misdemeanor, you can skip to the *Arraignment* section, as your case will not have an Initial Appearance, a Preliminary Hearing, or a Grand Jury Hearing. If you are charged with a felony, you should review the next section, which discusses the Initial Appearance and the Preliminary Hearing.

INITIAL APPEARANCE AND PRELIMINARY HEARING

If you were given a complaint charging you with a felony, the first hearing will be an Initial Appearance in the *Municipal Court*. The *Municipal Court* only has jurisdiction over felony cases for up to 15 days (or ten days, if you are in jail). At the initial appearance, you should enter a plea of Not Guilty and address bail.

Within 15 days (or within ten days, if you are in jail), the second court appearance will be a 'Preliminary Hearing' in *Municipal Court*. In theory, the purpose of the Preliminary Hearing is for the judge to determine whether the case should be bound-over to the *Common Pleas Court*, which requires the prosecution to prove there is probable cause to believe you committed the offense.

In practice, Preliminary Hearings are rarely held. Instead, when you appear for the Preliminary Hearing, the case in the *Municipal Court* will likely be dismissed. You will be informed whether your case has already been presented to a Grand Jury or will be presented to a Grand Jury in the future. Either way, the case in the *Municipal Court* is dismissed, and further proceedings will be held in the *Common Pleas Court*.

If an indictment was issued by the Grand Jury before the dismissal in *Municipal Court*, it is considered a dismissal with a 'direct indictment'. If an indictment was not issued by the Grand Jury before the dismissal in *Municipal Court*, it is considered a dismissal for possible 'future indictment'.

GRAND JURY HEARING

In Ohio, felony cases must be presented to a Grand Jury. A Grand Jury is a body of nine people from that county who are randomly selected to serve. At the Grand Jury Hearing, a prosecuting attorney presents evidence to the Grand Jurors. The evidence may include live testimony, or the evidence may be only written reports and exhibits.

You do not have the right to be present at the Grand Jury Hearing. You can be subpoenaed to testify at the Grand Jury Hearing, but you have the right to decline testifying (the right against self-incrimination). You do not have the right to have your attorney present at the Grand Jury Hearing.

After hearing the evidence, the Grand Jury decides whether you will be charged with the alleged offense(s). For you to be charged, the prosecution must prove there is probable cause to believe you committed the offense(s). If at least seven of the Grand Jurors vote in favor charging you (a 'True Bill'), the Grand Jury issues an Indictment.

An Indictment is a document notifying you that you have been charged with the offense(s). The indictment will be delivered to you, either with an arrest warrant or a summons for you to appear in court for an arraignment.

Note: In some felony cases, the officer does not serve you with a complaint. Instead, the officer submits an investigation packet to the County Prosecutor's Office, which prosecutes cases the *Common Pleas Court*. If the officer does not serve you with a complaint, you will not appear for an Initial Appearance or a Preliminary Hearing in the *Municipal Court*. Instead, you will receive an indictment, and your first hearing will be the Arraignment in the *Common Pleas Court*.

ARRAIGNMENT

The first court appearance in the *Common Pleas Court* is the Arraignment. The date and time of the Arraignment is listed in the summons which is served with the indictment. At the Arraignment, you will be given the choice of entering one of three pleas: (1) guilty; (2) no contest; or (3) not guilty.

You should give serious thought to what plea you will enter at the Arraignment. Pleading *guilty* is a complete admission of your guilt, and the judge will enter a finding of guilty. Pleading *no contest* is an admission of the facts alleged in the indictment, and, if the indictment is properly prepared, the judge will enter a finding of guilty.

If you plead *guilty or no contest* at the Arraignment, you will soon be sentenced, the case will be over, and you will not have the opportunity to defend yourself. If you plead *not guilty* at the Arraignment, you will have an opportunity to review the evidence against you, present evidence in your favor, and defend yourself against the accusation(s).

Some people worry that pleading not guilty will lead to a harsher sentence if they later plead guilty or are later found guilty. Generally, that does not happen. Judges understand you must plead not guilty at the Arraignment so you can at least review the evidence and evaluate the strength of the prosecution's case.

At the Arraignment, the judge will set bail. Bail is an amount of cash, property, or a bond which must be posted for you to be out of jail while the case is pending. The purpose of bail is to ensure your appearance at future court proceedings. When setting bail, the judge may also impose bail conditions. Common bail conditions include remaining in the state or county, refraining from contact with the victim's family, and not operating a vehicle.

At the arraignment, your attorney should address the appeal of the Administrative License Suspension (ALS). However, if the judge orders you to not operate a vehicle as a condition of bail, a successful ALS appeal will be in vain.

DISCOVERY

Discovery is the process of exchanging evidence between the prosecution and defense. To initiate the discovery process, your attorney should file a *Demand For Discovery*. The information you receive in the discovery from the prosecution will likely include:

- accident investigation report
- accident reconstruction report
- Electronic Data Recorder report
- arrest report and officers' narratives
- witness statements and your statements to the officer
- alcohol/drug influence report and field sobriety tests report
- Drug Recognition Evaluation report
- Administrative License Suspension report
- test results from blood/breath/urine tests
- expert witness reports
- medic reports and hospital records
- Coroner's report and death certificate
- photographs and videos
- your criminal/traffic record and criminal record of witnesses

In addition to filing the *Demand For Discovery*, your attorney can obtain evidence through records requests and subpoenas, such as:

- traffic camera videos
- surveillance videos
- police station and jail videos
- recordings of 911 calls and communication among officers and dispatchers
- medic run sheets

- documents and recordings associated with the Coroner's report
- maintenance records for the breath-testing machine
- breath-testing machine operator permits
- laboratory records for blood and urine tests
- permits for the laboratory technician and lab director
- personnel files of officers
- policies of law enforcement agency
- policies of Coroner's office
- policies of forensic laboratory
- reports of traffic conditions
- reports of weather conditions
- medical records
- cell phone records
- vehicle defects and recalls

If your case involves a blood or urine test, your attorney should file a *Demand for Testimony* of the laboratory technician who performed the blood or urine test. If this demand is not filed, the test report will be admitted as evidence without your attorney having the opportunity to cross-examine the laboratory technician.

When your attorney files a *Demand For Discovery*, there is an obligation to provide reciprocal discovery to the prosecution. The reciprocal discovery should include a list of potential defense witnesses and any evidence you may introduce in the event there is a trial.

The discovery process takes place primarily between the Arraignment and the Pretrial Hearing. Most prosecutors' offices provide discovery in two parts. The first part is written materials, and the second part is video and audio recordings. Depending on what office is prosecuting your case, what law enforcement agency was involved, and the extent of the discovery materials, receiving discovery can take anywhere from a few days to several weeks.

If you are represented by a lawyer, the discovery will be delivered by the prosecuting attorney to your lawyer. Your lawyer should then share the discovery with you. At the Dominy Law

Firm, we share each piece of discovery electronically as we receive it. We then schedule meetings or phone conferences with our client to discuss the discovery, evaluate the case, and make recommendations.

PRETRIAL HEARING

The second court appearance is the pretrial hearing. In some courts, it's called a status conference, and in others it's called a discovery conference. Regardless of the name, the purpose of the pretrial is for the prosecution and defense to discuss the case and negotiate toward an agreed outcome (plea agreement/plea bargain). If you reach an agreement at the pretrial, you may go before the judge to finalize the agreement.

If you are serious about improving the outcome of the case, your case will probably not be finished at the pretrial. I once had a judge say, "Shawn, you don't have a track record of resolving cases at the pretrial", to which I replied, "That's because the prosecutors don't have a track record of making good offers at the pretrial."

It's true. At some pretrials, the prosecution has not reviewed or provided all the evidence. Even if the evidence has been reviewed and provided, the plea offer at the pretrial hearing often is not favorable for two reasons.

First, prosecutors prefer to have a conviction for the most serious offense, so they offer a plea to that offense. For example, the prosecutor may dismiss a minor offense like Failure to Control in exchange for a guilty plea to vehicular homicide. If the defendant is willing to accept that, the prosecutor is very satisfied. The case is resolved without much work, and the prosecutor gets the conviction they want.

Second, if the plea offer is not accepted at the pretrial, it does not have an immediate effect the prosecutor. When the defendant rejects the plea offer, another hearing is scheduled, and the prosecutor is done with the case for that day. Prosecutors are typically dealing with many cases each day, so it is common for them to focus on the short-term goal of getting through the day's cases.

Unfortunately, many of the people who plead not guilty at the arraignment turn around and plead guilty to most serious offense at the pretrial. In most cases, to find out if the offer may get better, you need to go to the next stage of the case: the motion hearing.

Seven Steps for Evaluating Plea Offers

Deciding whether to accept an offer for a plea agreement cannot be reduced to a mathematical equation, but going through these seven steps will help you make the decision.

1. *What is the best-case scenario?* The best case scenario is a not guilty verdict or dismissal and no punishment.
2. *What is the likelihood of the best-case scenario?* Based on your attorney's thorough assessment of the prosecution's case, your defense, and the jurisdiction, predict the likelihood of obtaining a not guilty verdict. Naturally, this prediction is an art and not a science.
3. *What is the worst-case scenario?* A guilty verdict and the anticipated sentence that follows. Knowing the anticipated sentence requires familiarity with the judge's sentencing inclinations from prior cases, from reputation, or from representations made by the judge regarding this particular case.
4. *What is the likelihood of the worst-case scenario?* Because you and your attorney have assessed the strength of the case and predicted the likelihood of a not guilty verdict, you can also predict the likelihood of a guilty verdict. This evaluation is, of course, limited by the difficulty of predicting what verdict a jury will reach. It's more difficult in some cases than others.
5. *What is the certain scenario of the proposed agreement?* Assuming the agreement is approved by the judge, this is one factor in the evaluation that is known.
6. *Determine your risk tolerance.* Some clients are more risk averse than others.
7. *Analyze the factors in steps 3-6.* Compare the worst case scenario and its likelihood to the proposed settlement, taking into account your risk tolerance. Determine if it's better to have the certain outcome of the proposed agreement or better to try for the best case scenario, taking into account the possibility of the worst case scenario.

MOTION HEARING

When evidence is suppressed, it is thrown out (excluded) and cannot be used at trial. Based on what your lawyer finds in the discovery, your lawyer should probably file motions to suppress evidence. Many specific motions may be filed, but most of them fall into one of these categories:

- Motions to suppress evidence based upon search and seizure law
- Motions to suppress evidence based upon the Rules of Evidence
- Motions to suppress field sobriety tests
- Motions to suppress breath/blood/urine tests
- Motions to suppress your statements

Your lawyer also should have filed a motion appealing the ALS and a motion to terminate the ALS. Although the ALS is first addressed at the arraignment, the hearing for the ALS is usually postponed and held at the same time as the hearing for the motions to suppress evidence.

At the motion hearing, just before the hearing starts, there is typically a last- minute negotiation. This stage of the case is often the first time the prosecution takes a close look at the evidence and engages in meaningful negotiations. This stage of the case is also the first time the prosecution's witnesses need to appear in court. If there is a significant chance that evidence will be suppressed, and/or if there is a significant chance that you may be found not guilty in a trial, the plea offer typically improves. You usually need to get to this stage of the case to find out what is really the 'final offer'.

If you do not accept the prosecutor's offer, a motion hearing will be held. At the hearing, the officer(s) and any other prosecution witnesses will testify about what they observed and what they did. You or your attorney will have the opportunity to cross-examine the prosecution's witnesses, and you also may call defense witnesses. Each side then argues to the judge about what conclusions should be reached from the evidence. The judge issues a decision on the motions, either verbally (immediately following the hearing) or in writing (at a later time).

Motion hearings 'separate the men from the boys'. Although many lawyers have some understanding of the issues raised in motion hearings, few lawyers have extensive experience conducting motion hearings. Cross-examining witnesses and making legal arguments is an art, and one's mastery of that art improves with experience.

Just as you would not want your surgery to be your doctor's first, you do not want your motion hearing to be your attorney's first. You will want to find out which attorneys have experience and success in motion hearings. The prosecutors know who those attorneys are. They also know which attorneys are just bluffing when they file motions to suppress.

At the Dominy Law Firm, we have experience and success with motion hearings. In every case, we conduct legal research, file motions to suppress, and prepare to litigate the motions. We enjoy motion hearings (and trials): cross-examining witnesses and making arguments is one of the best parts of practicing criminal defense. Another great part is helping clients improve case outcomes. That's why we do not represent clients who intend to plead guilty. We only represent clients who are pleading not guilty with the goal of improving the case outcome.

Case Example

A police officer came into contact with our client. The officer smelled the odor of an alcoholic beverage and observed glassy/bloodshot eyes, so he administered field sobriety tests. The officer arrested our client, and our client's breath test result was .163.

We had a motion hearing on the admissibility of the breath test and the field sobriety tests. Cross examination revealed the police department did not comply with the regulations for maintaining the breath-testing machine, and the arresting officer did not comply with the protocol for administering sobriety tests.

The judge suppressed the breath test and all three field sobriety tests. At a later date, minutes before the jury trial was to begin, the prosecutor dismissed the charges.

TRIAL

If your case is not resolved at the motion hearing, it will be scheduled for a trial. You have the right to a trial, and you can choose to have a jury trial or bench trial. In a jury trial, a group of eight people (misdemeanor) or 12 people (felony) decides whether the prosecution proved your guilt. In a bench trial, a single judge makes that decision.

The trial has multiple parts. First is jury selection. After the jury is seated, each side gives an opening statement. The prosecution witnesses testify, the defense witnesses testify, and the prosecution may call rebuttal witnesses. Following the witness testimony, each side makes closing arguments. The jurors then retire to the jury room for jury deliberation (discussing the evidence) until they reach a unanimous decision. When the jury deliberates, they begin with the presumption you are not guilty. They can only render a guilty verdict if all the jurors agree the prosecution proved your guilt beyond a reasonable doubt.

The majority of vehicular homicide cases do not go to trial. In most cases, the prosecution and defense make similar predictions about the likely outcome of a trial, so they reach an agreement. The cases which do go to trial are often cases in which the prosecution and defense have very different predictions about the likely outcome of the trial. Other cases go to trial because the client absolutely cannot afford the consequences of the plea offer and has nothing to lose by having a trial.

It is important to choose a defense lawyer with trial experience. Imagine you are taking a flight on a commercial airline. You ignore the flight attendant's presentation about safety, and you don't give any thought to the pilot's qualifications, because there are rarely problems with commercial flights. If there is a problem, however, you want a pilot with skill and experience flying the plane.

If you were charged with vehicular homicide, there is a problem, so you want a lawyer with skill and experience handling your case. That experience must include trials, as prosecutors know which lawyers have trial experience and are therefore ready, willing, and able to take cases to trial.

SENTENCING

If you plead guilty to an offense, or if you are found guilty in a trial, the judge will hold a sentence hearing to determine what punishment to impose. The sentencing may be held on the same day as the guilty plea or trial, or it may be held separately, on a later date.

At the sentence hearing, the prosecutor may make a recommendation regarding the sentence, and your defense attorney will make a statement on your behalf. The judge will ask if there is anything you would like to say on your own behalf before the sentence is imposed.

When you speak, the judge does not want to hear excuses. If there is a legitimate explanation for the accident that does not form a complete defense, it is fine to share that explanation. Generally, however, it is best to acknowledge you made a mistake, accept responsibility for your mistake, and indicate you will make efforts to avoid making that mistake in the future. It also is beneficial to express remorse for the distress you caused to the victim's family. Give thought to what you will say, but don't memorize a speech.

After hearing from the prosecutor, the defense attorney, and you, the judge announces the sentence. Judges have wide latitude in what sentence to impose. For example, in an Aggravated Vehicular Homicide based on OVI, the judge can impose as little as two years in prison or as much as eight years in prison. The judge will consider factors such as prior convictions, the result of the blood/breath/urine test, your acceptance of responsibility, and other mitigating factors.

Knowing that most cases conclude with a Sentence Hearing, it is wise to develop a plan for sentence mitigation at the beginning of the case. That plan may include paying restitution to the victim's family. You should coordinate efforts with your insurance company and the lawyer representing you in the civil lawsuit. It would also be beneficial to undergo an assessment to determine if counseling is recommended, and then follow any counseling recommendations.

PART FIVE: MAKING DECISIONS ABOUT YOUR CASE

SHOULD I PLEAD GUILTY OR NOT GUILTY?

Before you go to court for the Arraignment, you will need to decide whether you will plead Guilty or Not Guilty. To make this decision, you should consider what happens if you plead Guilty, what happens if you plead Not Guilty, and whether it is worth the cost and time to try to improve the outcome of the case.

If you plead Guilty, the judge will impose the sentence, and you will serve that sentence without ever reviewing the prosecution's evidence. You cannot change your mind later. If you plead Not Guilty, you will have an opportunity to review the evidence against you, assert defense(s), and present mitigation. By pleading Not Guilty, you give yourself a chance of improving the case outcome.

The case outcome will not get worse by pleading Not Guilty at the Arraignment. Judges and prosecutors understand you must plead Not Guilty if you want the opportunity to review and evaluate the evidence.

In most cases, evaluating the evidence and preparing a defense leads to a better outcome. There are usually factual and legal issues which, if properly presented, convince the prosecutor to offer a more favorable plea agreement. There are sometimes issues which lead to the case being dismissed or result in a Not Guilty verdict. There are instances, however, when there are no weaknesses in the case which lead to a better outcome. As the outcome will not get worse, pleading Not Guilty has much potential upside and little potential downside.

At the beginning of your case, you should define what is a 'win' for you. A win for most people is obtaining a better outcome than the result which would have occurred by simply pleading Guilty. Once you define your win, you can address the remaining questions:

- Should I hire a lawyer?
- Are all defense lawyers the same?
- How do I choose a good defense lawyer?

SHOULD I HIRE A LAWYER?

To decide if you should hire a lawyer, you should evaluate how much you understand the legal and scientific issues, how familiar you are with court procedures, and how well you speak in public. You should take into account whether your case is a misdemeanor or a felony. You should also know whether you intend to plead Guilty or Not Guilty.

If your case is a misdemeanor and you intend to plead Guilty, you may not need a lawyer. I, personally, would still hire a lawyer in these circumstances. Like a tour guide in a foreign country, the lawyer can guide you through unfamiliar territory, explain what to expect, and warn you of dangers. The lawyer can also answer your questions, prepare court paperwork, and speak on your behalf at your hearing.

If you intend to plead Not Guilty, and/or if you are charged with a felony, you should hire a lawyer. Representing yourself is like treating your own medical problem. You can read about your medical problem on the internet (or at the library - remember those?), but if you need surgery, you should go to a doctor with expertise in that type of surgery. Likewise, you can read about legal and scientific issues online, but if you are going to effectively contest the charge, you should go to a lawyer with expertise in vehicular homicide defense.

A defense lawyer should be familiar with the Rules of Evidence, Rules of Criminal Procedure, Ohio Revised Code sections, Ohio Administrative Code sections, and cases interpreting all those laws. Good defense lawyers also have a firm understanding of field sobriety tests, blood/breath/urine tests, drug recognition evaluations, and accident reconstruction.

The lawyer must create a defense strategy, support it with motions to suppress, and communicate convincingly in negotiations with the prosecutor. A good defense lawyer also must be accomplished in the art of examining witnesses, making arguments to a judge, and presenting a case to a jury.

If you decide to hire a lawyer, you are probably wondering if all defense lawyers are essentially the same.

ARE ALL DEFENSE LAWYERS THE SAME?

If you are an NFL team owner, does it matter who plays quarterback for your team? Although all the NFL quarterbacks are good - they made it to the NFL- some are better than others. The same is true with lawyers. Although all lawyers made it through law school, some are better than others at vehicular homicide defense.

The skill of the quarterback matters so much that Kansas City Chiefs quarterback Patrick Mahomes is paid $45 million per year while (former Buckeye) Dwayne Haskins of the Pittsburgh Steelers is paid only $850,000 per year (how can he survive on that?!). In vehicular homicide cases, the skill of your lawyer matters too.

To be skilled at vehicular homicide defense, a lawyer must be proactive: law schools do not teach vehicular homicide defense. To achieve expertise in defending clients charged with vehicular homicide, a lawyer should start with independently reading all the relevant court decisions related to vehicular homicide and OVI, as well as all the statutes, rules and regulations. Next, the lawyer should learn about accident reconstruction, forensics, field sobriety testing, breath testing, blood and urine testing, psychology, sociology, persuasion, and litigation. Finally, the lawyer needs to put that knowledge to use in court by litigating motion hearings and jury trials.

As you can see, there is a lot to learn and experience to be a good vehicular homicide defense lawyer. It is practically impossible to develop expertise in this area while practicing other areas of law. For this reason, it is generally not a good idea to be represented by the family friend who handles divorces or business transactions but is willing to 'help out' with your case. Just as you would not go to your general practice doctor for brain surgery, you should not go to a general practice lawyer for vehicular homicide defense.

In Central Ohio, there are only a handful of lawyers who have developed expertise in vehicular homicide defense. Those attorneys get better results for their clients. The lawyers who don't put in the work to develop expertise often commit the 'seven deadly sins' of vehicular homicide defense.

The 'Seven Deadly Sins' of Vehicular Homicide Defense

1. *Overlook the importance of investigating quickly*. The defense investigation must begin soon after the accident. Evidence may be lost or destroyed, and the crash scene conditions may change. Witnesses may become unavailable, and their memories may fade. A private investigator or accident reconstructionist should take photographs, video, and measurements of the scene. A private investigator should interview witnesses. The lawyer should gather records and contact your insurance company.

2. *Ignore relevant records*. The evidence should not be limited to what the prosecutor provides in discovery. A defense lawyer should issue records requests and subpoenas to obtain other evidence which may impact the case. That evidence includes: videos from traffic cameras and the police station/jail, 911 calls, communication among officers and dispatchers, medic run sheets, medical records, breath-test machine records, laboratory records, personnel files, policies, traffic conditions, weather conditions, cell phone records, and vehicle recalls.

3. *Neglect to timely file motions to suppress evidence*. If the lawyer does not file motions to suppress evidence by the deadline, all the prosecution's evidence will be admissible. If the lawyer files the motions by the deadline, the lawyer gives you a chance of getting evidence excluded.

4. *Fail to challenge the accident reconstruction*. The prosecution's accident reconstruction will conclude you caused the accident. The lawyer should not simply accept that conclusion. The lawyer should hire an independent accident reconstructionist to challenge the accident investigation and reconstruction.

5. *Assume the rules were followed for chemical tests*. To determine whether the government complied with state regulations to make the blood/breath/urine test admissible, the lawyer needs to review law enforcement records that are not provided in the discovery process. Sadly, few attorneys review these records.

6. *Give up too early*. Most lawyers plead their clients guilty in the early stages of the case, so they never find out if the offer

would have gotten better by reaching the next stage of the case: the motion hearing.

7. *Take on too many cases*. Many defense lawyers handle a high volume of cases (usually for a low fee) and spend little time on each case. Those are the lawyers who plead their clients guilty early in the process without doing all the work necessary to put their clients in a position to improve the outcome of the case.

HOW DO I CHOOSE A GOOD DEFENSE LAWYER?

If you have a serious medical condition, the likelihood of overcoming the condition increases if you are treated by a good doctor with expertise in that condition. If you are charged with vehicular homicide, the likelihood of improving the case outcome increases if you are represented by a good lawyer with expertise in vehicular homicide defense.

The following tools will assist you in finding a good defense lawyer:

- Resources for researching lawyers
- 10 traits to look for in a defense lawyer
- 11 questions to ask about a defense lawyer's practice
- 12 questions to ask about a defense lawyer's qualifications

Resources for Researching Lawyers

Ohio Supreme Court: Every attorney in the state of Ohio is required to register with the Ohio Supreme Court. You can verify that a prospective attorney currently is licensed to practice in Ohio, and you can determine if the attorney has been disciplined by conducting an attorney information search.

Avvo.com: Avvo® is a website designed to help consumers research attorneys. The site contains profiles of most attorneys in Ohio, and each attorney is given a rating between 1.0 and 10.0. The profile contains the attorney's resume and includes client reviews and peer endorsements. You can search for attorneys by practice area and geographic area on the page titled 'Find A Lawyer'.

Lawyer Directory Websites: There are many websites which have lawyer directories. Some of them are for all types of lawyers, and some of them are for defense lawyers. Most directories are not very valuable because they do not really tell you objectively who the best lawyers are. The exceptions are: Super Lawyers®, Martindale-Hubbell®, and Best Lawyers in America®.

10 Traits to Look for in a Defense Lawyer

1. *Focus*. Choose a lawyer whose practice is focused on defense of serious vehicular crimes. There are hundreds of lawyers who will represent you in central Ohio. Most of them, however, also practice other areas of law. If you were having foot surgery, would you hire a family doctor with a general practice, or would you hire a foot surgeon?
2. *Expertise*. Select a lawyer with expertise in vehicular homicide defense. Many lawyers know the basics, but few have a deeper understanding of the legal and scientific issues in these cases.
3. *Experience*. It is necessary to have knowledge and expertise, but it is also important to have experience. Just as you do not want your surgery to be your doctor's first, you do not want your case to be the first one in which your lawyer argues a motion to suppress evidence or presents a case to a jury. Hire a lawyer with both expertise and experience in vehicular homicide.
4. *Service*. Choose a lawyer who provides good customer service. The number one complaint about lawyers is they do not communicate well with their clients. Your lawyer should keep you updated regarding all developments in your case, provide you with documents related to your case, and answer all of your questions. You can expect better service from a lawyer who accepts fewer cases rather than a lawyer with a high-volume practice.
5. *Personality*. You should find a lawyer with good people skills. If your lawyer does not interact well with you, how is he or she going to interact with the prosecuting attorney, the judge, and the jury when advocating for you?
6. *Industry recognition*. Select a lawyer who is recognized by his or her peers as a leader in serious vehicular crimes defense. Those lawyers often are asked to teach other lawyers at continuing education seminars. Those lawyers are also often se-

lected for Super Lawyers® and Best Lawyers in America®. In addition, peer reviews are available on Avvo.com.

7. *No guarantees.* In vehicular homicide cases, it is impossible for a lawyer to predict with certainty what will be the outcome of your case. To properly evaluate a case, a lawyer must review all the evidence, relevant law, and many other factors. All the evidence in a case will not be known until discovery is exchanged and the investigation is completed. Do not hire a lawyer who guarantees a certain outcome in your initial consultation.
8. *Results.* Choose a lawyer who has a history of obtaining good results for clients. A lawyer should be willing to publish, or at least share with you, the results of cases similar to yours. Hire a lawyer that has a proven record of results.
9. *Client satisfaction.* Find a lawyer who has satisfied clients. Client testimonials are available on many lawyers' websites. An even better source, Avvo.com, is an independent third party that collects reviews from clients and rates lawyers. Hire a lawyer with high ratings from previous clients.
10. *Appropriate fees.* Select a lawyer who charges appropriate fees. You can find inexpensive representation, but a lawyer who charges low fees for vehicular homicide defense either does not intend to do all the work necessary to present a good defense or does not have the expertise and experience to get good results. A low fee may also indicate what the lawyer thinks about the value of his or her service.

Remember the discussion of quarterbacks Patrick Mahomes and Dwayne Haskins? They both provide the same service, playing quarterback, but Patrick Mahomes is paid 50 times as much as Dwayne Haskins because Mahomes has a proven record of good results. A lawyer with expertise and a proven record of good results is going to charge higher fees than a lawyer without the same expertise and results.

11 Questions to Ask about a Defense Lawyer's Practice

1. Where did you go to law school, how long have you been practicing?
2. Please give me an overview of your career.
3. Have you ever been disciplined as an attorney?
4. To what professional organizations do you belong?
5. How many vehicular homicide cases have you handled?
6. How many new clients do you accept each month?
7. How many cases do you have pending currently?
8. How do you communicate with your clients and how frequently?
9. Will you provide me with everything you receive and file for my case?
10. Where can I read reviews about you, other than your website?
11. How much is your fee and what does it include?

12 Questions to Ask about a Defense Lawyer's Qualifications

1. What percentage of your practice is serious vehicular crimes defense?
2. Are you a member of the National College for DUI defense?
3. What do you do to improve your skills as a defense lawyer?
4. Are you ever asked to teach other lawyers?
5. What are the relevant laws and manuals for field sobriety testing?
6. How do the breath-testing machines in Ohio work?
7. What is your strategy for challenging breath/blood/urine tests?
8. What role does search and seizure law play in vehicular homicide cases?
9. What role does *Miranda* play in vehicular homicide cases?
10. How will you contest the accident reconstruction?
11. How many times have you cross-examined officers?
12. How many times have you examined expert witnesses?

CONCLUSION

You made a great decision to read this guide. Unlike most people charged with Vehicular Homicide, you are not in the dark.

You now have the information you need before going to court. You understand the types of vehicular homicide charges and their possible consequences. You are familiar with the evidence in vehicular homicide cases and the possible defenses. You also know what to expect in the court process.

This guide has provided the information you need before making decisions about your vehicular homicide case. You have a framework to help you decide if you are going to plead Guilty or Not Guilty, and a guide for deciding whether you want a lawyer. If you choose to hire a lawyer, you have resources for researching lawyers, criteria to evaluate their qualifications, and questions to ask when you speak with them.

Don't be the victim of a defense lawyer who takes your money and provides ineffective representation. There are only a handful of lawyers in central Ohio who have the expertise, experience, and other qualifications discussed in this guide.

Use the resources in this guide, do the research, and don't be afraid to ask questions. You will make well-reasoned decisions about how to handle your vehicular homicide case, and you will find a lawyer with the qualifications to improve the outcome.

ABOUT THE AUTHOR

Shawn Dominy, Attorney At Law

I have practiced criminal defense since 1997. In 2002, I began proactively developing expertise in serious vehicular crimes. I joined the National College for DUI Defense and completed specialized training in areas such as field sobriety testing, breath testing, and blood/urine testing. I also purchased the breath-testing machine used by most Ohio police departments so I could experiment with it.

The more I learned about serious vehicular crimes, the more I enjoyed this area of law. I continued with specialized training and gained extensive experience by taking hundreds of cases through contested motion hearings and jury trials. I now teach lawyers about OVI, serious vehicular crimes, and trial skills at state and national seminars, and my articles have been featured in state and national publications. I am listed in Best Lawyers in America® and named by Super Lawyers® as one of the top 50 lawyers in Columbus.

My firm limits the number of cases we accept so we can work each case thoroughly and give every client the service and attention we would want as a client. We only represent clients in Central Ohio courts (Franklin County, Delaware County, and their contiguous counties), and we only represent clients who intend to plead Not

Guilty.

Based on our expertise, our experience, and the level of service we provide, my firm's fees are often higher than the fees charged by other attorneys. We offer flat fees, so clients know the exact amount of the fees up front.

You can learn more about vehicular homicide and my law firm on our website and our blog. If you finish your research and would like to discuss representation, you can schedule a free phone consultation by email or by calling the Dominy Law Firm at 614-717-1177.

PRAISE FOR AUTHOR

"The Ohio Vehicular Homicide Guide is an outstanding handbook for anyone facing this serious charge. Shawn Dominy's clear and concise approach educates the reader about this complex area of the law. More important, however, he guides the reader through the difficult choices inherent in these cases. This is a go-to guide written by a go-to lawyer. Shawn Dominy is well-known for his ability in vehicular homicide defense, and it shows in this Guide."

- DAVID H. THOMAS, ATTORNEY AT LAW

"Shawn Dominy's guide for vehicular homicide is a valuable resource for people facing such charges, and it is also helpful for attorneys. The guide takes complex topics and relates the charges, penalties, and the process in an easy-to-understand and straight-forward manner. If you or someone you know is facing such a charge, this guide is worth reading."

- MICHAEL J. STRENG, ATTORNEY AT LAW

"After fifteen years of representing clients charged with various criminal offenses, I know vehicular homicide cases are, by far, the most devastating for all parties involved. Attorney Shawn Dominy does an incredible job of dissecting the complexity of the charges and simplify-

ing the process of strategically crafting a defense. For a person charged with vehicular homicide, this book is a must-read. Understanding both the nature of the charges and the process involved will certainly ease the mind of those facing the potential consequences associated with this alleged crime. For other attorneys, this book is an outstanding resource to better grasp the essentials in defending individuals charged with the same or similar offenses. Bravo, Mr. Dominy, for yet another exemplary product."

- ANDREW S. BAKER, ATTORNEY AT LAW

"Individuals facing vehicular homicide charges often find themselves exposed to the judicial system for the first time in their lives. They are submersed in an unfamiliar and stressful setting while being exposed to legal and technical jargon that can make no sense to the untrained. They are asked to make decisions that will have a substantial impact on their lives without knowing and fully understanding their rights involved. The Ohio Vehicular Homicide Guide removes much of this uncertainty. It takes the reader through the legal process step-by-step, clearly and concisely, from the time of initial contact with law enforcement through the court process and jury trial. This book should be primary source material for anybody facing these types of charges and for all attorneys handling these cases."

- VICTOR WHITNEY, ATTORNEY AT LAW

Made in United States
Orlando, FL
04 November 2026

90203673R00060